NE[...]

NEWTON, MA 02459

How To Be A Money Smart Student!

WITHDRAWN
NEWTON FREE LIBRARY

By

Brian Hostick

copyright 2012

332.024
H79H
2012

A partnership between American Library Association
and FINRA Investor Education Foundation

FINRA is proud to support the American Library Association

Dedication

This book is for my family. You're the
reason I do everything I do.

Table of Contents

Being a Money Smart Student – 1

Finances – 7

Education and Campus Life – 17

Housing and Transportation – 25

Food and Groceries – 31

All The Rest – 41

Personal Finance Resources - 51

1
Being a Money Smart Student

I'm writing this book so you don't end up like me. My financial problems came a little later in life but the foundation, or lack thereof, began much earlier – right after college earlier. It is a path taken by too many people. Excessive credit card debt, more and more money taken out in loans, irresponsible money management and poor control over expenses and spending. It eventually led to bankruptcy and the total destruction of my credit rating.

As I was getting my financial house back in order, I researched all I could about personal finance. I listened to the money gurus, and read all the blogs I could find. I realized two things - a) I wasn't alone in what had happened and b) it was happening to people at a younger and younger age all the time. In fact, it was obvious that teenagers were in dire need of a financial wake-up call.

The lack of a concentrated effort to teach students the importance of good financial habits is costing students money. According to USA Today, one out of every five people filing for bankruptcy is a student. The 18 -25 age group is the fastest growing demographic filing for bankruptcy. The Sallie Mae Foundation reports the <u>average</u> student will graduate from college with $25,000 in student loan debt and another $3,400 in credit card debt. The majority of students with credit cards will max that card out, regardless of the limit, before the end of their first year away at school. A lack of financial education is also costing colleges and universities large numbers of students. The National Center for Education Statistics reports almost 25% of all first year students will not return for their second year of college and over 40% of them are leaving because of financial issues.

It's understandable why things are the way they are with personal finance education. School districts are increasingly strapped for money themselves. Much of the focus these days has to be on core subjects which students need to go on to college or get through life in general. Extra courses are pushed aside, including classes which deal with money.

That leaves the task of teaching good financial habits to a student's parents. However, many parents are having their own problems in these difficult times figuring out how to take care of their own money matters, let alone pass on some solid knowledge to their teens.

A recent survey found that

approximately 70% of teens would like to learn their financial basics from their parents. Unfortunately, only 40% of parents in the same survey felt they were qualified, or were willing, to teach their teens about smart money management. That's a sizable gap in the want/need of the teens and the desire/ability of the parents when it comes to financial education.

If schools can't teach money classes, and parents can't or won't teach financial management at home, where are today's teens going to learn even the basics about handling their finances when they leave home for college, or venture out on their own?

It appears the responsibility is going to end up with the students themselves. The good news is, in my research, I've realized most teens *want* to learn how to handle their money. They know that there's more to it than just getting a paycheck from somewhere and paying it all out to various places. With a little guidance, a few tips here and there, and plenty of resources at their fingertips – today's teens can still be Money Smart Students!

This book is the 'few tips here and there' part. Some of the tips will also contain resources – all of which are listed together at the end of the book. My hope is that students who read this book will take it upon themselves to find out all they can about being money smart.

My father told me a saying a number of years ago - "If it is to be, it is up to me!" That is exactly the attitude students today need to take when it comes to their finances. Find out everything you can about money management. Read the multitude of blogs online dealing with this subject. You can find a list of the best personal finance blogs at www.wisebread.com.

I hope you will read through this book in it's entirety. All it will take is two or three tips to save you some significant money. If you save a total of just $200 dollars a month from the information you read in this book, it will add up to over $5,000 by the time you finish a three year college program. That's less money to borrow, or that you need to save on your own.

Thank you for getting this book and taking charge of your financial future. Use this, and every other resource you can get your hands on, so you can be a Money Smart Student.

2
FINANCES

Apply, Apply, Apply

Put your application in for any, and all, scholarships, bursaries and grants you can find. You never know what you could qualify for and who is giving away money for school.
That little $100 gift from the local Lions Club or Church Woman's League is a couple of week's worth of groceries!

Deadlines! Deadlines!

Along with applying for any and all scholarships – make sure you pay close attention to the deadlines on the applications.
You are guaranteed to receive none of the money you apply for after the deadline. Also – don't stop applying for money after you get into college. It isn't just Freshmen who get scholarships and bursaries. One of your part-time jobs in college should be to research and keep applying for scholarships – unless you are independently wealthy and don't need any help with your college expenses.

Only What You Need!

If you find you need to borrow money in order to pay for college, only borrow what you absolutely need. Take a hard look at what your expenses will be, how much you have saved, how much you may be getting from parents, scholarships, etc., and only borrow the absolute minimum necessary to cover your expenses. If you borrow more than you need you'll end up spending it anyhow. It will just mean that much more you will have to pay back – with interest.

A Little Here, A little There

If you do end up getting student loans, pay off whatever you can, whenever you can. Putting even the smallest amount down on your student debt, while still at school,will save you hundreds of dollars in interest in the long run. If you have a part-time job you should definitely budget a small amount of every paycheck for debt reduction.

Stay at Home

Sure, it would be great to go off on a wild trip to Mexico or Florida for Spring Break, but you better be using saved money and not student loan funds. Is it really worth all the interest you'll be paying to take a trip which will be a distant memory before you even start paying for it?
Stay local – visit family and friends – the sunny South will still be there once you graduate.

Emergency! Emergency!

One of the best things you can do for your own peace of mind is to set up an emergency fund before you head off to college. Put aside a small amount of money - $300 to $500. Save this money before you go away. Put it somewhere not easily accessible - maybe a savings account not attached to any bank cards. Use it only in case of emergencies – such as unexpected trips home or laptop repairs. By not having instant access to the money, you won't be tempted to spend it on 'emergencies' like the pizza man.

Track It!

Keep track of where your money is going. Keep all your receipts and bills for at least a month (October is a good one to use since you'll be settled into your new routine by then) and see where your funds were spent. You'll see where you need to cut back on spending and it will be easier to say 'No' to waste.

No Fees Please!

Be sure to check with your bank, or financial institution, to see if you are getting student rates on your accounts. Most banks and credit unions have 'no-fee' accounts for students. They know if you start your financial life with them you'll stay with them after you graduate. If you are getting charged fees on your bank accounts – you need to find another bank!

Home Sweet Home Branch

When taking money out of ATM's, only use the machines of your own financial institution. If you use another bank's ATM, you'll usually get charged double fees – one by the ATM provider and one by your own bank. If there isn't a home bank ATM near you, think ahead and use the 'cash back' service at major retailers such as Walmart. Get an appropriate amount of cash back when you make a debit purchase to last you until you can get to your bank or home ATM.

Plink! Plink!

Save your coin daily. You'll be surprised how fast it adds up. Use it for a special night out with friends once a semester. You can relax knowing it's not affecting your budget.

The Credit Card Menace!

Let's face it – credit cards are almost a necessity in this day and age. Online purchases, reservation confirmations for travel, you name it and a credit card is needed to do it. Having said that – being able to control your credit card use is of utmost importance to you as a student. Studies show 70% of students with credit cards will MAX OUT that card before the end of their first year – regardless of the limit! Only use your card when absolutely necessary. You should only have a credit card if you can get it before you go to college. Don't sign up for the cards which are promoted on campus. The long term pain, and interest you'll pay, isn't worth the free t-shirt to sign up.

No Balance!

If you do have a credit card – make sure you pay the balance off in full every month. The charges you are putting on the card should be in your budget, so you should have the money to pay them off in your bank account every month. DO NOT take cash advances out on your credit card. You get charged interest from the moment that money leaves the ATM and touches your hands. Credit cards can be a useful financial tool if properly managed.

Watch the Web

Be sure all your bank accounts are accessible online. It makes it so much easier to see how much money you have, any automatic payments that have come out, or gone in, and possibly any errors or fraud if you can instantly access your banking information. Most financial institutions are setup for this – if yours isn't, maybe it's time to get into the 21st century!

Smart Meters?

Find out if your utilities are cheaper based on the time of day. Many cities are switching over to Smart Meters which charge a different rate depending on what time of day the service is used. If electricity costs less late at night or on weekends, wait until then to do the laundry or run the dishwasher.

Right on Time

Be sure to pay all your monthly utility bills on time. You will save late charges and many companies will report late payments to the credit bureaus, affecting your credit score.

It's How Much?

Finally, make sure to read utility bills closely each month. Look for new fees, or charges which are much higher than previous months. If you don't understand a charge – call and ask what it is. This is true with any bill – electricity, cable, etc.

3

EDUCATION AND CAMPUS LIFE

Start Small

Attend a much less expensive local College to get General Credits before moving on to University to specialize. Just be sure to check that the course credits are transferable and recognized by the University.

Testing! Testing!

See if any of your courses have a 'test out' option. If you already know the information from outside studies, you can save a bit of money on tuition and textbooks by getting the class credit through taking one test instead.

Software Solution

Many colleges and universities have distribution licenses with the major computer software companies. Find out if you can get a copy of any needed software from your school and save money in download purchases.

Share and Share Alike

If your school doesn't have software licenses, try to use 'open' or shared computing tools such as 'Open Office'. Most, if not all, of the features are the same as the name brand software and it's available FREE online.

Refill Please!

According to the Chicago Sun-Times, over 300 million ink jet cartridges are thrown into landfills every year – the equivalent of 30,000 elephants in weight. If you have your own printer for your computer, get ink cartridges refilled instead of buying new every time they run out. Whether you do it yourself, or take it to a specialty ink jet refill kiosk, you'll be saving money and the environment by topping it up instead of replacing.

Final Copy Only

The same Sun-Times report says if you filled the average vehicle's gas tank with printer ink instead of gasoline, it would cost you around $175,000! To save on that expensive printer ink, make sure you do all editing and proof reading of assignments on the computer screen. Only print out the final copy of a paper to hand it in. This will save ink, paper and wear and tear on your printer.

Really?

As soon as you know your courses and have your book lists, email your professors to see if you absolutely must have all the books. Some books are listed just to end up being used for reference and some are used so rarely they could be shared with other students. At over $100 each, cutting out one textbook a semester could mean saving $800 by graduation time.

Buy and Sell

There are numerous sources online when it comes to buying and selling used college textbooks. If you want to keep it local, list your texts on Kijiji, or look there to find books from students who took your course in previous years. Just make sure you are buying the same edition used in class. International editions may have different questions and review sections. Don't immediately sell your books back to the campus bookstore. You'll only get pennies on the dollar compared to what you paid.

Work On-Campus

If you're looking for a job while at school, keep your eyes open for employment on-campus. Whether it's the bookstore, or the computer lab, jobs in colleges and universities are usually very flexible with hours. Sometimes you can do homework while on the job, and it's not exactly back-breaking labor. Besides, you'll meet lots of your fellow students and make some money at the same time.

Get Involved!

When not working, or studying, get involved in campus life. The more time you spend volunteering your services, or taking part in charitable events, the less time you will have to spend money doing something to just fill up your time. This includes finding a charity you support off-campus and giving of your time and energy there.

There are also numerous free activities taking place on college and university campuses on a daily basis. Maybe it's a special seminar on a subject you're interested in, or a free concert in the Arts department. Keep an eye on the bulletin boards and postings around campus for events of interest and keep yourself busy with some fun stuff.

Get a Job!

If you think you can handle it, get a part-time job of any kind while at school. Studies show students with part-time jobs get better grades because of the extra organizational skills needed to pull it off. A little extra spending money never hurt anyone either.

Leave Fido at Home

If you're moving away for school, leave your pet, or pets, at home with family. Pet food and Veterinarian bills can add up throughout the year.

4

HOUSING and TRANSPORTATION

Sabbatical Savings

If you are responsible, and don't plan on having any wild parties where you live, see if there are any professors you know who are going away on sabbatical leave. If their house was going to sit empty anyhow, maybe they'll appreciate someone taking care of the place while they're gone in exchange for either free, or reduced rent.

Residence Savings

If you are gong to be living on-campus, apply to be a student resident adviser. In exchange for overseeing what goes on in residence, and helping people out with their problems, you could get cheap, or free, room and board. This also looks good on job applications because it shows responsibility.

Meet the Roomies

Hold off on making any large item purchases for your residence until you meet your roommates. You never know what they might be bringing with them.

Huddle Up!

If you are living off-campus, and are sharing a house or apartment with roommates, hold a regular monthly money meeting. This will put everyone on the same page when it comes to sharing expenses and will save on headaches throughout the school year.

Program Savings

If your landlord allows it, get a programmable thermostat for your house or apartment. Turn down the heat/air while everyone is in class and warm it up/cool it down just before classes end for the day.

The Closer the Better

When searching for off-campus housing, look as close as possible to school. Being within walking or biking distance can mean hundreds of dollars in savings versus driving. There are no parking fees, gas costs or maintenance. Plus, you'll feel better and be saving the environment.

Take the Transit

If you must find housing further away from campus - make sure you are near a main bus line to school. Again, there are savings in getting a student bus pass versus driving. If you bring your car to campus you'll just end up being taxi driver for all of your friends.

Hitch a Ride

If you are moving away to go to college, so are other people from your area. Search out students from your home city through bulletin boards and see if you can car pool for trips to and from home.

Everybody chipping in a bit for gas is cheaper than four different vehicles all traveling the same way with one person in them.

Maintenance Saves Money

If you are going to take your vehicle away with you to school, stay on top of it's regular maintenance schedule. Oil changes, tire rotation and other regular repairs could save you a major repair bill in the future. It should also go without saying to make sure your insurance is always up to date and in effect.

Compare Prices

Before you fill up, go online and check the latest gasoline prices on sites such as www.gasbuddy.com. If gas is less expensive outside of your regular in-town traveling area, and you can make it there on the fuel you have, you can save throughout your years at college by getting gas on the cheap.

I Know A Guy...

Almost everybody knows 'a guy'. If you need something fixed in your apartment, or someone to look at your laptop which is acting up, ask your friends if anybody knows 'a guy' (or a girl!) who can help. It could be worth some savings - as long as you are sure the repairs will be done properly.

5
GROCERIES
AND FOOD

No Name = Low Price

Almost all major grocery retailers these days have their own 'store' brand of food. Whether it's canned goods, dry goods, or snacks – you can find the generic brand of almost any item right beside the name brand version on the same shelf. Take a close look at the prices. The store brand item will almost always cost less – much less except if the name brand is on sale.

Savings can be found in the 30-45% range on some items, and that adds up over time. You can either spend less – or buy more food for the same amount of money you would have spent anyhow on name brands.

If you buy $120 worth of groceries every two weeks, and you save 25% overall by buying as much as possible in generic items – you'll save over $2,000 during the length of your stay at school.

Waste Not – Want Not

A couple of tips working together here. First – make a menu of what you are going to have for meals for the coming week. This includes lunches and dinners, since you will be eating both every day, either at home or in the school cafeteria. Second – make a detailed grocery list of what you need to buy to make those meals on your menu. Making a grocery list cuts down on impulse buying since you will only get food you need – not what you see on the shelves that catches your eye. North Americans waste tons upon tons of food every year simply because it has gone bad in the fridge, or has passed the expiration date on the shelf. Control your impulse grocery buying and you'll save money.

Check the Label

Before you make your grocery list for the coming week, check the food you do have on hand. Look at the expiration dates to see if an item needs to be used up in the very near future. Plan your menu to include any ingredients which are soon to expire or need to be used shortly. Refrigerated items such as yogurt should be watched especially closely and consumed before they expire. Better to have a yogurt for lunch three days in a row than to throw them out in the garbage.

Learn to Cook

All of those first tips assume you are going to be cooking your own meals and eating at home. Don't be the typical student living on Instant Noodles five days a week. You won't need to if you budget properly, plan your meals, and learn to cook a few tasty staples. Learn some of your Mother's recipes the summer before you go away. Get some actual written recipes from Mom, or Grandma, and try them out on your roommates or friends.

Not having to rely on take-out food will save you hundreds of dollars a month. The ability to cook for yourself is a skill which will come in handy throughout your entire life. Start the learning process now.

Make a Bit Extra

If your recipe can handle it, try to make a big enough batch of your food so you can have leftovers. Save the leftovers in proper storage containers in the fridge. Plan on having the leftovers for lunch the second day after they were made. This way it won't seem like you're having the same food meal after meal. This will also save you money on buying food for lunch.

How Cold Can You Go?

To properly preserve your carefully purchased food, or leftovers, make sure your fridge is set to the proper temperature. The thermostat should be set between 35-38 degrees F in the fridge, and right at 0 in the freezer. Keep your food at the right temperature to avoid spoilage and waste – and thereby money.

Oldie But a Goodie

It's an age old saying which has been around for years – but it has been proven to be absolutely true. Don't go grocery shopping on an empty stomach! You will buy food you don't need just to eat right away and take away that hungry feeling. You'll buy bigger sizes of products and you'll be in a hurry so you'll forget to follow your list – or the fact you may have some coupons for some items. Have lunch first if shopping on the weekend. Wait until after dinner if you're going to the store after school.

Watch the Screen

Keep an eye on the cashier's screen when you are checking out at the grocery store. Be sure you don't get double dinged for any items, that all sale prices have come through properly, and that any coupons you may be using are credited correctly. We all know that people aren't perfect and mistakes happen. When you throw electronic devices into the mix anything is possible. Watch the screen.

Bread in Bulk

If you find bread on sale somewhere, buy a few extra loaves and throw them in the freezer. A half day to thaw one out while you're at class and it will be just like a fresh new loaf, at a nice cheap price.

Cut! Cut! Cut!

Recent television shows have shown the savings available through the use of store and manufacturer's coupons. While going to those extremes may not be feasible, it takes just a little time to browse through the newspapers for coupons on items you are going to be buying anyhow. Half a buck here, and a free item there, add up over time. Cut coupons whenever possible to save yourself some money or so you can afford something nice for a cheaper price.

Buy Local

If there is a farmer's market in your college area – attend it as often as possible to purchase your vegetables and fruit. Support your local businesses and you will find you get very good quality at competitive prices. Try to focus on getting fruit when it is in season. Fresh produce is better for you and tastes better than stuff that's been shipped across the continent.

Specials on Staples

When shopping, or looking through the flyers, watch for big specials on staples which won't go bad. Dry goods such as paper towels, and toilet paper are always good things to have plenty of around. Sugar and flour last a long time when stored properly.

Buy in Bulk – But Don't Buy in Bulk

There is no need to be buying five packs of romaine lettuce when you're a college student. It will just go bad before you ever have the chance to use it all up. Be smart when it comes to buying items in bulk. However, if you can share the savings of bulk purchases with a few friends – buy in quantity and split the items up amongst yourselves. Just make sure everyone agrees to the cost and who is getting what at the end of the grocery trip.

Take a Snack

Need a little pick me up between classes – take a healthy snack from home in your backpack. Avoid using the vending machines at school. The snack you bring will be much healthier and won't cost near as much as the machine.

Get With The Plan

If you are lucky enough to be on a meal plan at your college – USE IT! You're just wasting money by not taking advantage of this prepaid plan to feed you on campus. Don't waste money on takeout or too many groceries if you don't need them.

There's an App For That

As with most things to do with buying these days, there are numerous apps available to help you with your grocery shopping. You can make menus, which will then automatically give you the shopping list you need. You can scout out where all the food you need is located in your grocery store. 'Grocery Gadget' is one such app but there are lots more available for any operating system.

6
All The Rest!

Hit the Yard(Sales)

During the summer before heading off to school, scout out some local yard sales for supplies. Small furniture pieces, plates, utensils, cups and mugs are always in large supply at yard sales. Just make sure you thoroughly sterilize anything to do with eating or drinking before you use it.
Also – at the end of the school year, hold your own yard sale to get rid of items you can't take home with you. Might also be a good chance to unload a few textbooks.

Lose The Land Line

If everyone of the residents of your apartment have a cell phone, there really is no need for a land line is there? Make sure your 911 callback info is linked to your school year address, and not your home address, in case of an emergency.

B.Y.O.S.

If you are heading out to a laundromat to do your laundry, always take your own supplies and a bag of snacks and drinks. The cost of laundry detergent, dryer sheets and junk food at the laundromat is out of this world compared to what you can bring. Also – the machines at the laundromat are a lot bigger than the basic home model. Fill those machines right up to use less overall loads and save a little bit of cash in the process.

Free Is Good

Take a look at the 'Free' category under items for sale on your local Craigslist and Kijiji websites. You'd be surprised what people are willing to give away for free just to get it out of their house.

Entertainment not Spendertainment

When it comes to going out on the town, avoid going to places where spending money is the main activity. Casinos and race tracks can end up costing more money than first intended.
Along the same lines, don't go buying lottery tickets with student money. Make your own fortune by getting a good education!

Sports Party Central

For major sporting events – Super Bowl, World Series games, etc. - don't go out to a bar to watch. You'll spend way too much on marked up alcohol and food. Instead – organize a party at your place, or somebody else's, where everyone brings their own refreshments and snack foods are pooled. These are usually the kind of get together with friends you will remember for a long time.

Discount City

Ask <u>everywhere</u> you shop if they offer a student discount. Retailers in college towns know that students are their bread and butter. You'll be surprised how many stores will give you a student discount if you just ask.

Quit It!

I know sometimes it's easier said than done, but college is a great time to give up on your vices. Smoking and drinking can cost a lot of money over the course of your studies – but both you, and your bank account, will be healthier if you are able to kick the habits.

Cover Me, Dad!

Find out if you are still covered under your parent's health plan while you are away at college. If you are, don't pay for additional coverage through the school, or privately.

Healthy is Happy

You can't be at your studying best if you are feeling under the weather. Take care of your physical self to get through the school year healthy. Eat properly, get plenty of rest, and keep up with regular preventative health care such as Dentist appointments and flu shots.

Use My Teeth, Please

Speaking of dentists and oral hygiene, does your school train professionals in the dental care field? If so, they might need someone to volunteer their mouth for the students to do work on. See what you can find out about donating your mouth to dental education. It could mean cheap, or free, dental care while you're at school.

Snip Snip

If you're adventurous, get your hair cut by a Beauty School trainee. These schools usually offer deep discounts for people willing to put their hair on the line in the name of education.

Eye Care – You Care

If you need to get your vision checked while at school, look for an Optometrist attached to an eye wear store. You can usually get cheaper, or free, eye exams if you see the specialist and buy your glasses or contacts from the same location.

Be Safe

This is the most 'controversial' tip in this entire book. If you're going to fool around at school – practice safe sex! There is nothing like an unexpected little bundle of joy to throw a serious wrench in your financial plans, and your future plans in regards to college.

Thrift Store Heaven

Thrift Stores are a terrific source for low maintenance clothes and accessories. You can find some neat pieces of jewelry, as well as scarves and belts at great prices. If you've got time to look through the racks, you can find some great deals.

Some Quick Final One Liners

Make some extra money by offering your services as a tutor (for a fee of course)

Give services such as babysitting or lawn care as gifts instead of buying something.

Instead of going out – have a movie night in with friends. Do pot luck with snacks and bring your own drinks.

Getting a haircut at a national chain? Check their website first for money saving coupons.

Don't buy clothes which are 'Dry Clean Only'.

See if a membership to the campus gym is cheaper than going off-campus.

Use a water filter system instead of buying bottles. You'll save money and the environment at the same time.

Keep a stain remover stick in your backpack. It could save on cleaning costs, or replacement costs.

Your Own Ideas

-

-

-

-

-

-

Personal Finance Resources

www.moneysmartstudents.com

Join me on our home website for tons of student money information.

www.wisebread.com

A great website with an overall focus on personal finance. Wisebread.com (get it – smart money - wise bread!) also features a listing of the top 700 or so personal finance blogs on the internet.

www.moneywise.com

Moneywise.com contains numerous tools for personal money management. They have solutions in place to help you track your debt and ideas to help you get out of debt faster.

www.ewealthwatchers.com

The Wealth Watchers program follows the basic principals of another "Watchers' organization – promoting group support and regular meetings to help you manage your money. Founder Alice Wood has also written a book of the same name with lots of helpful tools.

www.collegefinancialaidadvisors.com

Founder Jodi Okun provides families with guidance and direct assistance in finding financial aid for college. The CFAA website is also a great resource when it comes to scholarships and other types of student financial aid.

www.gasbuddy.com

Great website for searching out the cheapest gasoline prices anywhere in North America. Save time and money using this resource before filling up.

www.fastweb.com

Search here for scholarship listings of all kinds.

www.scholarshipscanada.com

Source for Canadian students searching for scholarships and bursaries. Find financial aid listed by school, and source.

www.mint.com

One of the most powerful budgeting websites available. Mint.com will link all your accounts together, helping you manage your budget and debt. The tools also have the ability to be used from your mobile device.